PRINTED IN THE UNITED STATES OF AMERICA
10 9 8 7 6 5 4 3 2 1

ISBN: 978-1-943684-78-6 (HC); ISBN: 978-1-943684-79-3 (SC).

PUBLISHED BY 99 PAGES OR LESS PUBLISHING LLC.

WELCOME TO HORROR-LAND

Be Careful What You Wish For (Betrayed)

Death Certificate Belongs To:

____

____

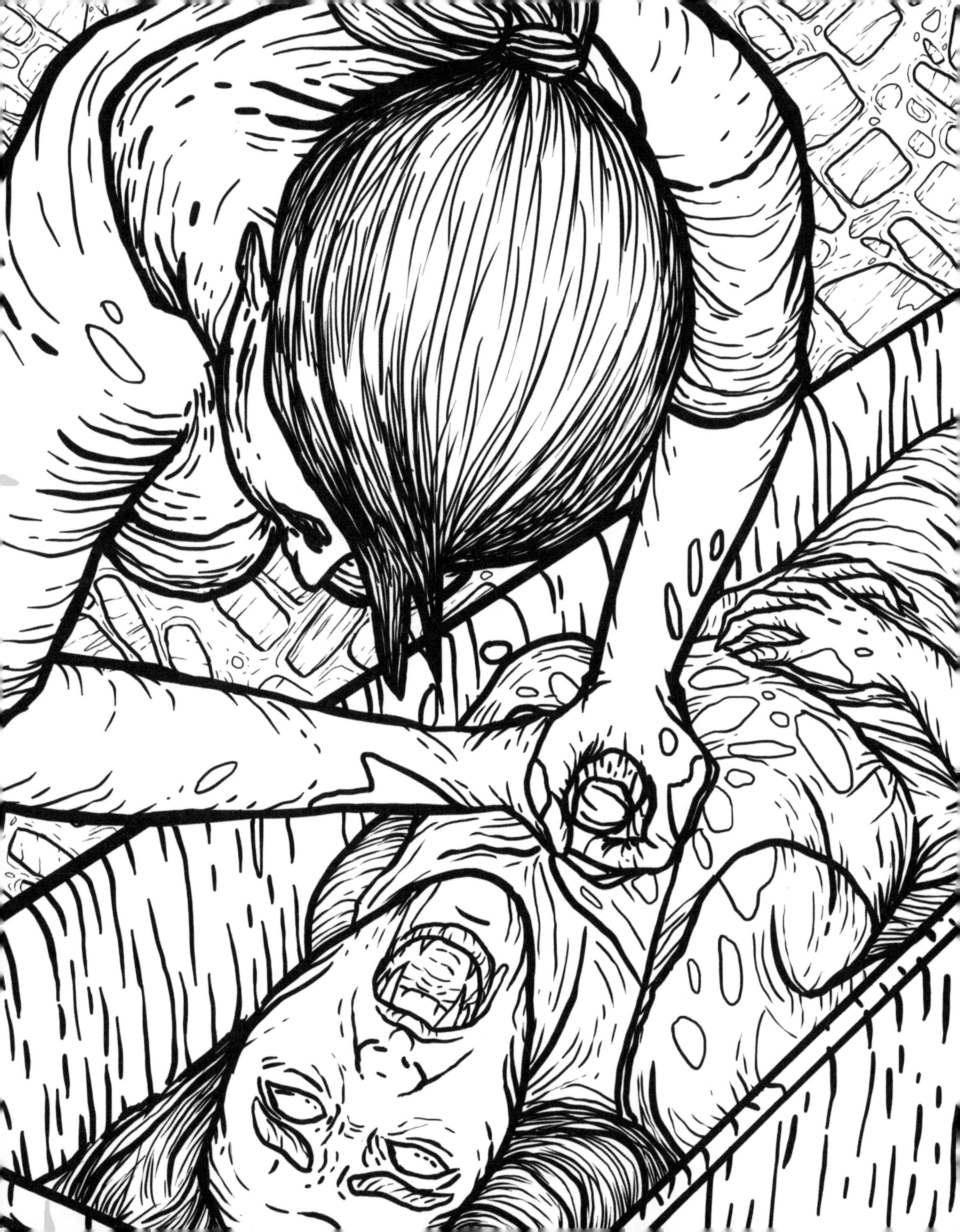

www.ingramcontent.com/pod-product-compliance
Lightning Source LLC
Chambersburg PA
CBHW080852190726
48292CB00011B/2966
* 9 7 8 1 9 4 3 6 8 4 7 9 3 *